The World of NASCAR

NASCAR Rules

by Gail Blasser Riley

Reading Consultant:
Barbara J. Fox
Reading Specialist
North Carolina State University

Content Consultant:
Betty L. Carlan
Research Librarian
International Motorsports Hall of Fame
Talladega, Alabama

Capstone press

Mankato, Minnesota

Blazers is published by Capstone Press,
151 Good Counsel Drive, P.O. Box 669, Mankato, Minnesota 56002.
www.capstonepress.com

Library of Congress Cataloging-in-Publication Data
Riley, Gail Blasser.
    NASCAR rules/by Gail Blasser Riley.
    p. cm. — (Blazers. The World of NASCAR)
    Includes bibliographical references and index.
    ISBN-13: 978-1-4296-1288-3 (hardcover)
    ISBN-10: 1-4296-1288-6 (hardcover)
    1. NASCAR (Association) — Juvenile literature. 2. Stock car racing —
Juvenile literature. I. Title. II. Series.
GV1029.9.S74.R55 2008
796.72 — dc22   2007022733

Summary: Describes the rules governing NASCAR racing, including safety and
racing rules.

Essential content terms are *bold* and are defined on the spread where they
first appear.

Editorial Credits

Mandy Robbins, editor; Bobbi J. Wyss, designer; Jo Miller, photo researcher

Photo Credits

AP Images/Gene Blythe, 15; Glenn Smith, 6
Artemis Images, 5
Brian Cleary/www.bcpix.com, 14
Getty Images for NASCAR/Rusty Jarrett, 16–17; Getty Images Inc./AFP/Brian
    Cleary, 7; Chris McGrath, 23; Robert Nickelsberg, 27; Scott Boehm, cover;
    Streeter Lecka, 22
The Sharpe Image/Sam Sharpe, 8, 12, 13, 18, 20–21, 28, 29
Transparencies, Inc./Sam Sharpe, 11

1 2 3 4 5 6 13 12 11 10 09 08

Table of Contents

Deadly Crash!

On February 18, 2001, NASCAR fans were enjoying the Daytona 500. With only one lap to go, everyone was on their feet. Suddenly, something went wrong.

On the final turn, Dale Earnhardt
lost control of his #3 car. He slammed
head-on into the track wall. At the
same time, he was hit by another car.
Earnhardt died from his injuries.

Sadly, Earnhardt's life could have been saved. A Head and Neck Support system (**HANS**) would have kept his head from crashing forward. Doctors think that is what killed him.

HANS — a system of straps that holds a driver's head in place in a crash

Dale Earnhardt Jr. wearing HANS system

8

After Earnhardt's death, NASCAR changed the rules. Now all drivers must wear the HANS system.

TRACK FACT!

Dale Earnhardt is tied with Richard Petty for the most points championships. They have both won seven.

Safety Rules

NASCAR is an exciting but dangerous sport. Rules protect drivers, crews, and fans.

The HANS system is one of the newest safety measures taken by NASCAR. Special seats and seatbelts also protect drivers during crashes.

driver wearing **HANS**

Drivers wear suits that protect against fire. Drivers also wear fire-safe boots and gloves.

Bobby Allison racing, 1986

TRACK FACT!

In 1987, Bobby Allison's car nearly flew into the stands when it crashed at high speed.

Restrictor plates were used on certain tracks by 1988. These metal plates limit the air and fuel that reach the engine. They keep speeds down and prevent deadly accidents.

official inspecting restrictor plate

ST. MARY'S SCHOOL LIBRARY
GARDEN CITY, KANSAS

15

pit crew changing tires

Safety rules also protect pit crews.
Crews wear fire-safe clothing, helmets,
and eye gear.

TRACK FACT!

During pit stops, only seven crew members can be over the wall. Other crew members hand items to them from the other side.

Talladega Superspeedway

Rules to Race By

NASCAR races are meant to test the skill and talent of drivers. NASCAR rules are made so that no driver has an unfair lead.

Limits are put on cars to control speed and *handling*. Cars may be tested for cheating at any time.

handling — how the car behaves on the track

TRACK FACT!

Drivers, owners, and crew chiefs can all be fined and punished for failing inspections.

Officials use many types of flags. Each flag sends a message to the drivers. When cars crash, the caution flag is waved. When this flag is out, drivers may not pass each other.

Green flag starts a race.

22

The goal in NASCAR seems simple: win the race. But scoring isn't that simple. Scoring rules give points to drivers for where they finish in each race.

Race Flags & Their Meanings

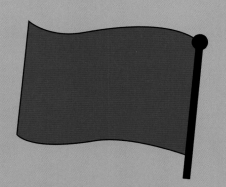

Green – The race is beginning or restarting after a break in the action.

Yellow – Caution. Slow down. There has been an accident, the weather is bad, or there is debris on the track.

Red – The race is stopping because of a large accident or weather-related issues.

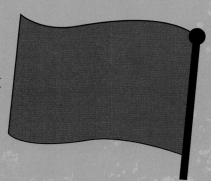

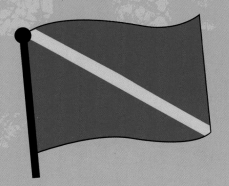

Blue with Orange Stripe – Pay attention to your mirrors. Move over for the faster traffic that is approaching.

White – There is one lap left in the race.

Black – Come into the pits. You are having a mechanical failure or have broken a rule.

White Cross on Black – Your laps won't be scored until you report to the pits.

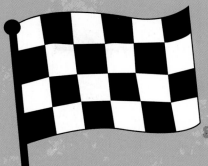

Checkered – The race is over.

Spreading the Word

Each year, NASCAR updates the rules. Drivers, crew members, and car owners each receive a rulebook.

The rulebook covers general
NASCAR guidelines. But each
racetrack may have extra rules.

Knowing and following the rules is very important. All drivers go to a rules meeting before each race. What if a driver misses the meeting? That driver starts the race in last place.

Glossary

handling (HAND-ling) — how a car behaves

HANS system (HANZ SISS-tuhm) — a system of straps that prevents the driver's head from snapping forward; HANS is short for Head and Neck Support.

inspection (in-SPEK-shuhn) — when something is looked over very carefully

official (uh-FISH-uhl) — a person who decides whether rules are being followed

restrictor plate (ri-STRIKT-ur PLAYT) — a device that limits the power of a race car's engine; the restrictor plate keeps down the car's speed for safety.

Read More

Brock, Ted. *Fast Families: Racing Together through Life.* The World of NASCAR. Excelsior, Minn.: Tradition Books, 2003.

Kelley, K. C. *NASCAR Authorized Handbook: All You Need to Know About the 2004 NASCAR NEXTEL Cup Series!* Pleasantville, New York: Reader's Digest, 2005.

Kelley, K. C. *Racing to the Finish: Teamwork at 200 MPH!* All-Star Readers. Pleasantville, New York: Reader's Digest, 2005.

Internet Sites

FactHound offers a safe, fun way to find Internet sites related to this book. All of the sites on FactHound have been researched by our staff.

Here's how:
1. Visit *www.facthound.com.*
2. Choose your grade level.
3. Type in this book ID **1429612886** for age-appropriate sites. You may also browse subjects by clicking on letters, or by clicking on pictures and words.
4. Click on the **Fetch It** button.

FactHound will fetch the best sites for you!

Index